This UK and Commonwealth Edition by
Schofield & Sims Limited Publishers ©1995
Series by Françoise Detay-Lanzmann
Text by Françoise Detay-Lanzmann and Nicole Hibert
Illustrations by Frankie Merlier
First published by Editions Mango, Paris ©1995

0 7217 5016 8

The Sea

Schofield & Sims Limited Huddersfield.

Oceans and Seas

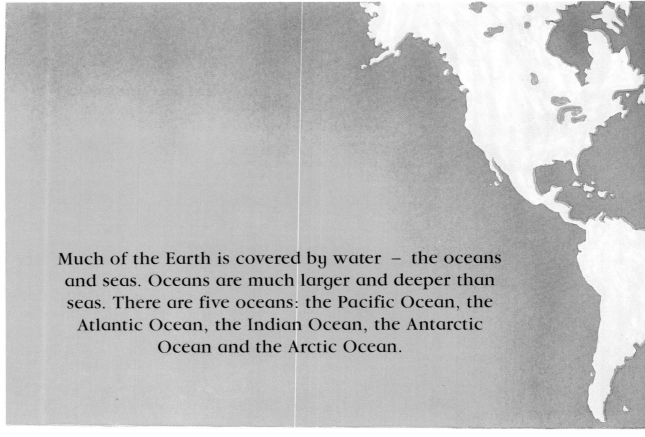

Much of the Earth is covered by water – the oceans and seas. Oceans are much larger and deeper than seas. There are five oceans: the Pacific Ocean, the Atlantic Ocean, the Indian Ocean, the Antarctic Ocean and the Arctic Ocean.

When an ocean is partly enclosed by land, it is called a sea. Inland seas, such as the Black Sea, are surrounded by land.

There are cold seas and warm seas. In warm, sunny parts of the world, it is possible to swim in the sea all the year round.

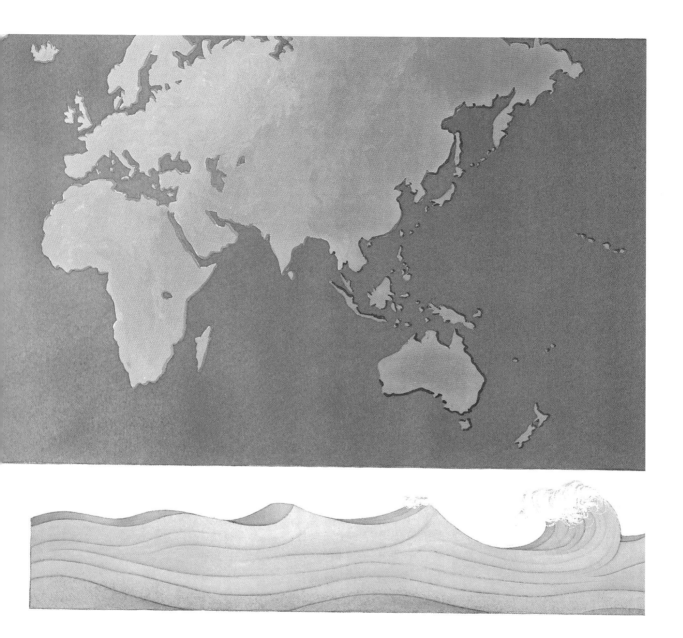

The ocean is always moving. On the surface, the waves rise and fall with the wind. Deep in the ocean, there are powerful warm or cold *currents* which are also created by the wind.

Underwater Landscapes

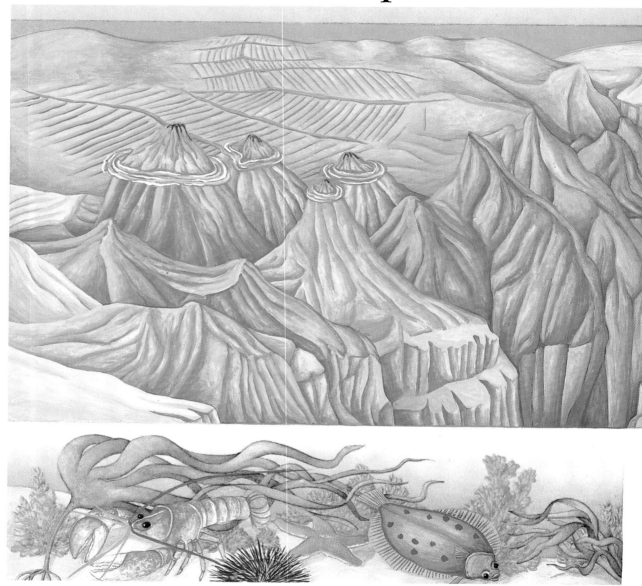

The water around the edges of the continents isn't very deep and is quickly warmed by the sun. Here, we can see sponges, starfish, lobsters, octopuses, and many kinds of fish.

The landscapes under water are very
varied, just like those on the surface.
There are vast plains and huge
mountain ranges, as well as many
volcanoes and *trenches*.

In the warmer waters, tiny animals called corals live in large groups or colonies. As
these animals die, their hard skeletons form huge coral reefs which give shelter and
nourishment to many species of beautifully-coloured fish.

The Coast

The coast is where the land ends and the sea begins.
Some coasts are steep with rocky cliffs.
Others are flat with sandy beaches. Dunes are hills of
sand which have been formed by the wind.

Some coastlines are jagged, with creeks, bays and coves separated by capes and
headlands. The pebbles thrown up by the waves wear the cliffs away. In time, the
cliffs will crumble and creep further inland.

The sea lapping against a cliff may wear away a hole that gradually grows bigger until it becomes a cave, then an arch. In some places, the coast advances into the sea because of the *alluvial deposits* carried there by rivers.

The Ocean Depths

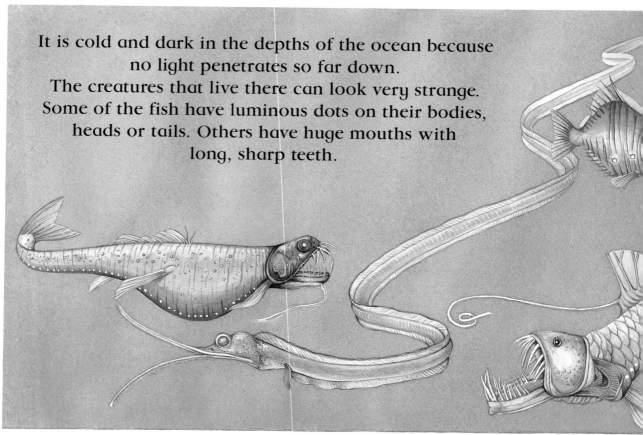

It is cold and dark in the depths of the ocean because
no light penetrates so far down.
The creatures that live there can look very strange.
Some of the fish have luminous dots on their bodies,
heads or tails. Others have huge mouths with
long, sharp teeth.

The giant squids that live among the
sea lilies have large eyes and long
tentacles, which they use to catch
tiny fish.

Sea lilies are actually animals, not
flowers. They have long, thin, feathery
tentacles, which they use to trap their
prey and carry it to their mouths.

Some rocks give off hot water and gases. The warmth makes these places important areas for the development of many sea creatures.

The angler-fish has a long, thin snout like a fishing-rod growing from its head, with tentacles at the tip. It uses this 'bait' to catch its prey.

Beaches

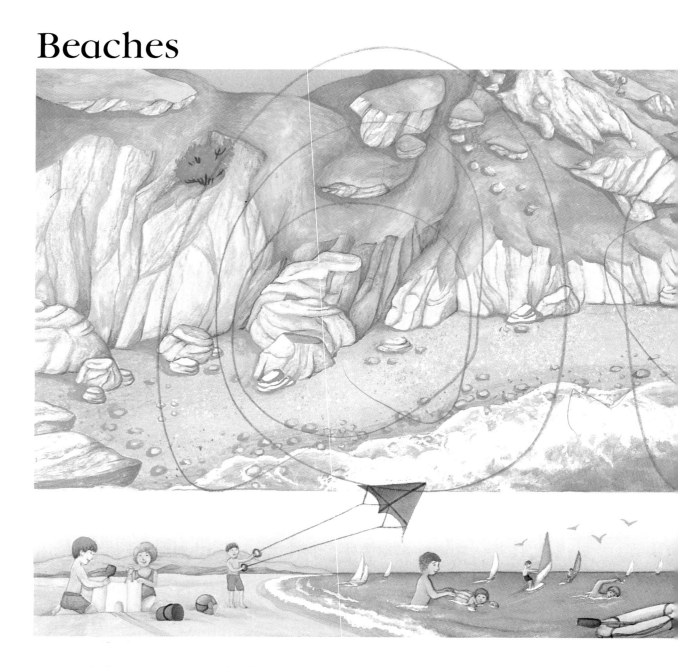

On sandy beaches we can build sandcastles, play with a ball, fly kites or collect shells. From the beach we can go sailing, surfboarding, windsurfing or swimming. The lifeguard keeps watch over the beach to make sure swimmers don't get into difficulties.

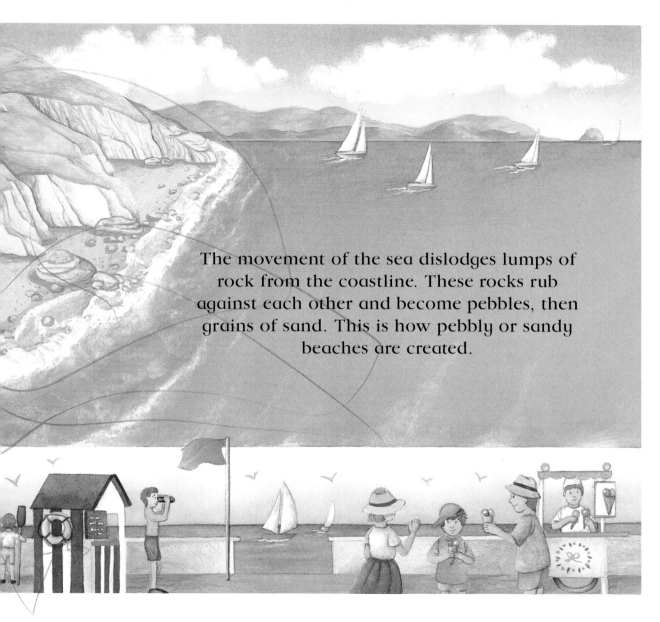

The movement of the sea dislodges lumps of rock from the coastline. These rocks rub against each other and become pebbles, then grains of sand. This is how pebbly or sandy beaches are created.

Before going swimming, it is very important to check the times of the tides and the colour of the flag. A red flag means 'Danger! Do not swim!' Swimming is allowed when the flag is green. It's very enjoyable to sunbathe so long as your skin is well protected and you wear a hat to avoid the risk of *sunstroke*.

Fish

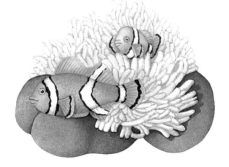

The clown fish lives inside the tentacles of the sea anemone, which protects it. The fish nourishes the anemone with the remains of its food.

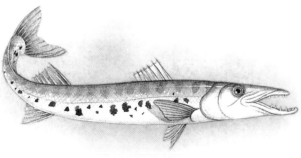

The fierce barracuda is known as the tiger of the sea. It has powerful jaws and is a savage hunter. Barracudas grow to over a metre in length.

There are thousands of fish of many
different shapes, sizes and colours. Fins
help a fish to swim and keep its balance.
The tail fin pushes the fish forward
through the water.

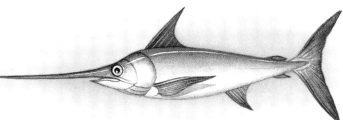

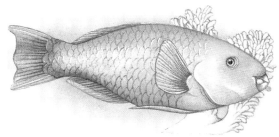

The swordfish uses its 'sword', a bony
extension of its upper jaw, to slash its way
through *shoals* of fish. It also uses it to
attack enemies – including fishing-boats!

The parrot-fish has a kind of hard
beak which it uses to bite off pieces
of coral. These fish are very
brightly coloured.

Fishing

Each year, fishermen all over the world catch millions of tonnes of fish. Modern fishing vessels have electronic equipment to help locate the *shoals* of fish.

Tuna is caught in different ways. One method uses special boats equipped with many long poles, from which hang several lines with bait.

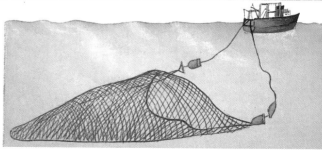

The trawler drags an immense funnel-shaped net, the trawl, through the water to catch fish such as cod, haddock and sole.

Some fishing-boats use a net called a seine, which looks like a huge draw-string purse. These nets are used to catch sardines and other fish that swim together in *shoals*.

Lobsters and crayfish are caught in wooden pots placed on the seabed. *Buoys* help the fishermen to find the pots.

Sea Birds

Many sea birds nest on cliffs and on small rocky islands, where they live in flocks that can often be very large. Gannets build huge nests using seaweed, feathers and grass.

The cormorant dives into the water to catch fish and crabs. Afterwards, it dries its feathers by spreading out its wings.

The puffin nests on the cliff top in a burrow, which it digs out of the soft earth and lines with grass.

The female guillemot lays a single, pear-shaped egg. The shape of the egg helps to prevent it from rolling off the cliff.

The delicate-looking storm petrel is the smallest sea bird. It flutters above the waves looking for *plankton* and fish, usually at night.

The Treasures of the Sea

There is oil under the seabed. To pump it to the surface, narrow wells are dug from platforms that are almost like floating towns. Gas is also extracted from beneath the sea.

Pearls are formed when a grain of sand becomes trapped in an oyster or mussel shell. A substance called *nacre* is secreted around the grain to form a pearl.

Salt is the sea's main treasure. Sea water is collected in shallow ponds called salt-marshes. When the water evaporates, the salt can be harvested.

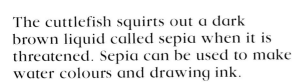

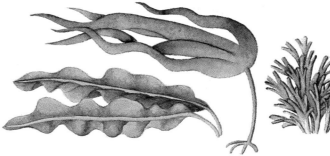

The cuttlefish squirts out a dark brown liquid called sepia when it is threatened. Sepia can be used to make water colours and drawing ink.

Seaweed has many uses. Some kinds of seaweed, such as kelp, are used as fertilisers. Other kinds are used in the manufacture of food and drugs.

The Sea in Danger

The seas and oceans of the world have become rubbish tips into which tonnes of harmful waste products and chemicals are dumped.

When too many fish are caught from the same area, it reduces the number of fish left to lay eggs. This means that fewer eggs will hatch and so there will be fewer fish to catch.

Sometimes a supertanker spills its load of oil into the sea. When this happens, the oil spreads over the surface of the sea and on to the shore, causing extensive pollution and killing thousands of fish, birds and mammals.

In the past, the blue whale was hunted almost to *extinction* for its blubber and its meat. Nowadays, we try to protect whales by limiting the numbers that can be caught.

Other sea creatures, such as the seal, the turtle and the puffin, are at risk because of pollution, hunting and fishing.

People and the Sea

In order to protect the sea, we need to understand it.
This work is done by scientists called oceanographers, who
study plant life and sea creatures.

Miniature submarines transport
people to work and study in the
ocean depths. They can stay
under water for about 10 hours.

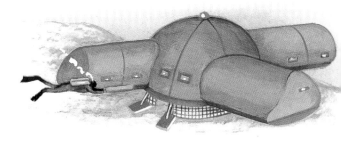

Nowadays, even houses are being built
under the sea! Here, scientists can live
and work for long periods whilst they
study life in the ocean.

Treasure is sometimes found on the seabed. Inside the sunken wrecks of ships, divers can find gold coins, jewels and cannon.

People have always liked to sail across the sea. Nowadays, fast sailing ships are built to race each other round the world.

Low Tide

Around the shores of the British Isles, the sea
rises and falls twice a day. This is called
the tide. When the tide goes out, we say
it is low tide.

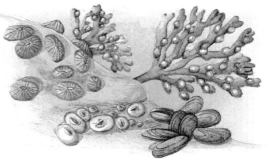

At low tide, pools are left among the
rocks where crabs, shrimps, starfish and
other small sea creatures live. Seaweed
is often found in the pools.

Some shellfish, such as barnacles,
limpets, mussels and whelks, cling to
the rocks when the tide goes out. Others,
such as clams, burrow into the sand.

Many different shells can be found in the sand. There are cockles, scallops, clams, cowries and razor-shells.

The oyster-catcher uses its powerful beak to open the shells of mussels, oysters and cockles.

Glossary

Alluvial deposit

A layer of fine soil left after a time of flooding, usually in a river valley or delta. It contains a lot of organic matter and is very rich and fertile.

Buoy

An object that rests on the surface of the sea to mark the position of something on the seabed.

Current

A large quantity of water or air flowing in a particular direction.

Extinction

The word used to describe when something no longer exists – when it has been completely wiped out or destroyed.

Nacre

A smooth, shiny substance made by oysters and mussels, which they use to line their shells. Nacre is often called mother-of-pearl.

Plankton

The tiny animals and plants that float in the top layer of the sea or fresh water.

Shoal

A large group of fish swimming together.

Sunstroke

A serious medical condition caused by staying out too long in very hot sun.

Trench

A long, narrow, sunken place or hollow on the ocean bed.